THE EFFECT OF THOUGHTS

SUKHMANPREET KAUR

Made with ❤ on the Notion Press Platform
www.notionpress.com

Contents

Contents

Contents

Contents

Contents

Introduction

The book contains 100 quotes from variant facets of life that primarily emphasis on the ideology of performing those tasks that we resist ourselves to perform. What and how we think about our lives is the focal point. The quotes in this book will inspire you to live your life accordingly. The book demonstrates that whatever the situation is, it should be dealt with positively in order to defeat it. It will remind you to show gratitude toward yourselves. This self-help book will re-energize your desire to be consistent and determined in your pursuit of your dream goal. Furthermore, it states that the actions should be directed in the right direction.

Inspire, and just be inspired,

Determine, and just be determined,

Achieve and be unbeatable,

Happy and just be happy.

Actually, this is something that life wants to make us realise all the time.

Adore life and enjoy reading.

CHAPTER I

Books are the best escort to listen to, and writing is the best companion who listens to us without whinging.

CHAPTER II

The most malignant thing is being overly reliant on everything.

CHAPTER III

3

Overthinking plays a reflective role in shattering your applauding thinking.

CHAPTER IV

You are better in other things as well, just explore.

5

Your inside spark should light up the perceptions in your brain.

6

Perfection can be even discovered in imperfection.

CHAPTER VII

You can be better than you think,
You can do better than as much you do.

Sometimes a scintilla is enough to move forward.

CHAPTER IX

Fantasy life and legitimate life have a thousand dissonances. Consequently, abstain from living a dream life.

Your life is your responsibility, because anyone cannot help you. You need to help yourself.

11

Poignancy takes you distant from reality.

12

The compound interest of happiness is irenic.

13

Your lack of effort is the most obvious sign of defeat.

14

Redundant joviality and superabundant desolation do not always remain.

15

Who is the burden of this world?
One who cannot stand out for itself.

CHAPTER XVI

Evade being a parasite who relies on others, there is nothing better than being self-subsistent.

17

It is a futile effort to force someone to do anything.

A good beginning or adverse beginning of the day does not determine how our entire day will unfold; it is entirely up to us.

Anyone cann't do anything without putting efforts.

CHAPTER XX

The most valuable skill we can cultivate is efficacious thinking.

CHAPTER XXI

Your extensive rivalry is your lividness.

22

There is always one person to give you back, and that is you.

23

Whimpering over every situation is not the solution; unfold the page and try to look for glee in other ways. A single thing is not the reason for jocundity every time.

CHAPTER XXIV

The logic behind recuperative mathematics is a secret, and it is that you have to solve all the catastrophes by yourself, and life's exigencies are just the same.

25

Do not think you are sluggish; your brain only does what you command.

CHAPTER XXVI

SELF NOTE

26

CHAPTER XXVII

Dreaming is not wrong; excess of everything is wicked.

28

I do not believe in magic, but one thing that none of us can overpass is that the magic of our hard work beats everything.

29

Edification from never-ending obstacles is the best part of life. Enjoy the process.

We feel good if we get something free of charge, nevertheless remember there is always some hidden cost for everything. It is "your time." So, just have a look. If you are spending your time somewhere, Is it worth it?

31

Level up regardless of your current position. Starting and rejuvenating the flow of that beginning will not make you feel distressed in the future.

CHAPTER XXXII

Voids of exhilaration can be filled up with your hard work, perseverance, and consolidating power.

CHAPTER XXXIII

To challenge ourselves is one of the best things I have discovered so far. The best thing to realize is that, only we know what we do, and having control over that situation is difficult. And, to challenge that laborious situation, is CHALLENGING OURSELVES.

CHAPTER XXXIV

If you feel stuck somewhere, do not try to give up there.
If you feel you are going to lose, do not try to give up on hope.
It might take days, months, or years, but remember, one day it will be yours for sure!

35

Left or right only matters in directions; this is not possible; it also matters in life, which pathway to choose. One should need to know the accurate difference between these two. Inbuilt this property inside you.

Frame a picture of your aim in life. Take a deep breath and reflect on your activities for the day. Also, keep a track of what you have accomplished. That is the simple rule to being trackable.

Inspire and get inspired—this is the perfect relationship we can have with the world.

Millions of people had variant experiences on this day; it could have been busy or productive; ordinary or extraordinary; it is up to us how and what we have experienced or learned from the day.

A reminder:
Credible ruminations always come from
good reading.

CHAPTER XL

On asking yourself a question, "What do you like to gift or reward yourself with?" Everyone will have a contrasting reward for themselves; however, I would like benefaction myself with strength just to implode every verge of limitation.

Assign yourself as the moderator of your life; no one can superintendence your arbitration about your life. One life gives you the contingency to enjoy it whole via having control on yourself.

42

Regardless of how energized your actions are, your vision and thinking should be broad as well.

*You have to understand this elegant
ideology: you are enough for yourself, no
matter how you look.*

Seeking perfection every time will not work; unplanned and unexpected events may take your entire day; however, they will teach you at least, by the end of the day.

45

Sometimes we have to give up on some things. We sometimes fail. It is okay. To achieve something, failures are crucial.

46

Being the latest version of yourself, according to the situation, will enforce you to do better.

47

Learning is all about gaining knowledge from various perspectives, nevertheless what about learning about your own worth?

48

Resist distractions; procrastination will impede your goal. When you have a cosy day, you will recklessly resist other unbeneficial activities.

For peace, do not seek here and there; it is empowered by God and is inside you.

Fall through as much as you want; nevertheless, abstain forgetting to learn from your failures.

The word "impossible" is just a piece of advice that you get from others.

SELF NOTE

52

53

Do not fictitious your smile; it ought to be natural.

"I WILL DO IT" is the phrase that will give you remorse in the future.

55

*You ought to work everlastingly in order
to have the day you desire.*

Your sentiments are tackled; that is why you are frustrated, and this will end up wasting your whole day.

57

All the impenetrable situations that we have encountered are noteworthy because they have taught us the superlative lessons of life.

58

Every day is a fortuitous one, as we all know; however, only 1% of people know how to use and incorporate that fortuity into their lives.

59

Learning different things trains your mind to stay healthy and fresh.

Create more opportunities to have more possibilities.

61

Try to stand on our own; there isn't always someone to back you up.

62

Know yourself better so that you can handle yourself in any situation.

Do a self-analysis to determine:
"HAVE I IMPROVED MYSELF OR NOT,
TO HAVE A BETTER DAY
TOMORROW?"

HARD WORK IS WHAT?

It is that a student does to be a topper.

It is what an aspirant does to crack a competitive exam.

It is what an office employ does for promotion.

It is what a businessman does to make an empire out of his business.

CHAPTER LXV

65

We presuppose the termination of something is perpetually compacted, although it is conspicuous for an inexperienced beginning.

Your success ladder is called "Small Progress Consistently."

CHAPTER LXVII

Life is fulfilled when we end up with no regret.

The most elegant thing in your life is you.

Your face never attracts anyone, but your body language attracts everyone.

A busy street gives you noise, but a busy, although productive, life gives you seemly success.

71

An irenic environment gives you serenity and a placid mind gives you success.

CHAPTER LXXII

72

A good book is like your good friend, and your good friend is like your good book.

73

WHAT ARE DRREAMS?
Dreams are those that never let you obliterate for what you concupiscence.

A person who has never falls down reflects that he/she has never accomplished anything significant in their lives. It is a universal fact.

75

Enjoy your life by overcoming challenges before life enjoys you by defeating you.

76

The optimum approach to subjugate any phobia is just to face it.

CHAPTER LXXVII

SELF NOTE

77

CHAPTER LXXVIII

78

Exigent times teach us how to stay serene in every situation.

79

Pushing yourself beyond your impedes is something one must learn.

You will always try to preclude having negative thoughts once you realize how influential positive thoughts are.

Every day is not gratifying, nevertheless, something satisfying often happens when you think positively about situations.

CHAPTER LXXXII

Differences are extensive, whenever you learn to distinguish between positive and negative thoughts, you will find a better way to reach your destination.

Control your thoughts because they dominate your life.

84

There is certain darkness required to see the star, and we must also face some darkness in our lives because it is obligatory.

85

The influential marks of a happy life are:
CREATIVE IDEAS AND POSITIVE
THOUGHTS.

Any contingency come in front of us twice in our life, it is not the rule.

87

The unforeseen acts are also the eventuality of our actions.

CHAPTER LXXXVIII

Which is more pivotal? HARDWORK OR SUCCESS! The hard work because it is indispensable for success.

Life teaches us many lessons, but if we move forward without learning the lessons, we will repeatedly come to that point from where we have started.

Without learning, it is not possible to reach the destination.

91

Both ACCESS and EXCESS have significant differences, but there is a vigorous connection between these two words: an EXCESS amount of education is required to ACCESS our dreams.

*The leading justifications for our defeat
are that:
We do not give ourselves a chance.
We defeat ourselves in our own minds.*

93

Covering up behindhand is better, than even not attempting a single task.

Consolidate your powers to upgrade yourself. Learn from an amateur who fights with himself or herself on a daily basis to be proficient.

95

We all want everything to be spongy but conjure up that spongy pathways lead to an intricate life.

96

Remember, the past has passed; it will never be a solution to anything.

97

We are limitless; it is just that we limit ourselves to perform any work.

98

The role of encumbrances is to teach what life is!

Impulsive accomplishment will not occur, but slowly and steady success will definitely happen.

The best views are always visible after going through the hardest ways.

Living with the exigency is not the solution; either leave it or solve it.

Stop looking for things to be settle in an order, start organizing them.

103

Fail today

But do not forget to rise tomorrow.

CHAPTER CIV

SELF NOTE

104

Short Note

Whenever there is a strenuous situation come, we lose courage to face off it, anything we face off, it seems hard all the time. The fear of anything, leaves an individual in the middle of the sea. The learnings we make through the hard times, these should need to motivate us and reflects in our mind, just like revising a flashcard.

To be motivated, persaude yourself
To be fearless, be valiant
To be unbeatable, be insormountable
Life is the **flamboyant journey,** *the justification behind this is:*

It teaches us the lessons, where we fail and step up.

TO ENJOY THE LIFE:
LIVE IT
AND
LIVE IN THE PRESENT.

Author Page

The author has been inspired to write since childhood, and her affectionism toward writing grows stronger with age. Sukhman started writing quotes in her diary with inspiration from her PARENTS. According to Sukhman, writing is the best companion. She is a self-published teenager author. This is the author's second book. She has already written a book called "Bond with the Reality of Life.

GET IN TOUCH WITH THE AUTHOR:
Mail address: Kaursukhmanr445@gmail.com
Instagram: @author_sukhmanpreet_kaur
Youtube: @author_sukhmanpreet_kaur
Contact number: 9646661691